LEAVES OF CLASS

Leaves
of
Class

Kit Robinson

chax
2017

Library of Congress Cataloging-in-Publication Data
Names: Robinson, Kit, 1949- author.
Title: Leaves of class / Kit Robinson.
Description: Victoria, TX : Chax, 2017.
Identifiers: LCCN 2016052330 | ISBN 9781946104038 (softcover : acid-free paper)
Classification: LCC PS3568.O2894 A6 2017 | DDC 811/.54--dc23
LC record available at https://lccn.loc.gov/2016052330

Chax Press / PO Box 162 / Victoria, TX 77902-0162

Chax Press is supported in part by the School of Arts & Sciences at the University of Houston-
Victoria. We are located in the UHV Center for the Arts in downtown Victoria, Texas. We
acknowledge the support of graduate and undergraduate student interns and assistants who contribute
to the books we publish. In Spring 2017 our interns are Julieta Woleslagle and Gabrielle Delao. Sophia
Kameitjo, a former intern, also assisted with the work on *Leaves of Class*. The book is also supported by
private donors. We are thankful to all of our contributors and members.
Please see http://chax.org/support/ for more information.

Thanks to the editors of the following publications in which some of these works have appeared:

*Boog City, Cannot Exist, Mary, On Barcelona, Shampoo, Spoon River Poetry Review, Sun's Skeleton, The
Nation, The New Hunters Review* and *Try.*

Chax Press thanks Karl Young for his artist's book pictured on the cover, *Second Series (Mining
Rainbows)*. The book is part of the collection of Charles Alexander, who photographed it for use here.

Dragons and elephants, give me your questions!

— Shunryu Suzuki

CONTENTS

Decima

for Elio Villafranca & John Benitez

For your teaching and musical direction
I want to thank you from my heart
Without you I would have been a lonely *tresero*
Neither piano nor guitar
You showed me the way to lay down the *montuno*
In solid *clave*, *guajira* style
And when we hit it our *descarga*
Was something I will not forget
Thank you my teachers for showing me the way
Thank you my brothers, you are true *compadres*

17 Reasons Why

My first thought is of the person, the one continuously organizing all of this, this
        … whatever-you-call-it

My second thought is, yes, let's try for something more, oh, I don't know, pointed?

My third thought is, since we're going to be here for a while, let's have some fun

My fourth thought is, maybe we should try to sweep the floor a little more often

No more thoughts at this time

I think I might of seen 17 Reasons once, or maybe it was just the sign

Au contraire, we are not language poets, we are *The Beast American* poets

Original Manny's. I seem to remember the T-bone is marinated in lighter fluid

My Invisible Man juice wore off when I realized the line snaked around clockwise and
        I'd have to push little kids out of the way to take a peek at Mars

Adult Male Victims of Recreational Injuries, ha ha

Yes, 4 is good, maybe even a little better than 12

I love it when Marie pretends to bang her head against a wall

Adios, Big Girl

The anxiety attack was the best part

On a bench by the new Claes Oldenburg bow & arrow monument in front of the new Gap
        HQ building housing the huge new Richard Serra sculpture at
        Embarcadero & Folsom

What big waves of art & commerce we've had!

Contingency rules! But then what else is new? Avast!

Aye, Marvelous Marvin. He had the great dry tone of steel-edged civility

Saw him recently on TV in *The Professionals* (1966), with Lancaster, Ryan, Bellamy & Strode
        as mercenaries rescuing Claudia Cardinale from Jack Palance in Mexico

Bellamy: You bastard! Marvin: In my case an accident of birth, but you, sir,
        are a self-made man. . .

The Big Sea

When I was a poet's poet
I used to be a musician's musician
Then a white cloud

Carried me away
and I got carried away
thriving on a phrase

No chorus
rings true
like air with a splash of water

Meaning that life
flickers on and off
in these words

A slight chill
from outer space
just before sunset

The sea is the color
of poetry
alive in air

An imaginary tune
breaks rocks
on the sound of time

My machine sings
because it is plugged in
this is my song

A view out over water
a sea of absolute difference
too much to take in at a glance

Flash Of The Spirit

after Robert Ferris Thompson

The woods and their medicines are grander than any document

The rivers and their denizens are statelier than any address

The flowers and their pollinators are busier than any bourse

The caves and their pools are darker than any vice

The clouds and their prevailing winds are more vague than any passing thought

The nerves sit ceremonious who say I am not home

The crossroads are inscribed on the wall with a magical marker

The signs of the times flicker on and off intermittently somewhere down the hall

A 48-story building with 2,500 squatters today in Caracas

Wake up and smell the salt water lapping at your heels

The freeways and buildings are more porous than any coral

The tablets and devices are more sensitive than any adolescent

The integration points are more open than any sluice gate or lock

The planetary currents and tides are more inexorable than any dialectic

The moon and stars are more distant than any second cousin twice removed

Shikantaza

I know what I'm doing
Ear eye nose and throat in working order
That's why they call it work
How sweet sweat is
When you draw a bead
Watching the river flow
Walk don't walk don't run

It's all happening right now
Soft belly   soft brow   soft tongue
Keep on keeping on, yo
It's all good   doesn't get much
Wide angle lens on
Soft rain   sleeping body   warm home
Neither move nor stay put

Just sitting
Legs hurt like hell
The day is a test of stamina
It's damn wonderful
If you don't get too distracted
Take it easy my friend
Take it *and* leave it alone

Loosely Coupled

Language is a body
Of thought resting
After coming

Same time same state
Plumes for miles
Reed combinations

Physical security
Remains in farce
Before dawn

Toenails are colorful
Sketches of rain
Write home

Whole body laughter
Wings of song
Open gate

Light lamp
Cool surface
Night sky

Time all around us
To end thinking

The Planetary Currents

We live on the third rock from the sun

In our living rooms

We handle the remote and touch off integrated circuits compelling content,
       non-integrated circuits such as the chitlin' circuit, and disintegrated circuits such
       as the extended family now stretched across six continents

Plus one under ice

The rapid flows of global capital

Put us to sleep and wake us

We come on in on a wing and a come on

We slide right across the ice

We stop to catch up, so like a breathing tree

We read in the wind a thin hint of the following message from our sponsors:

Instead of reading about the unconscious we decide to enter it, that is, by falling asleep

Dream of a document signed by CEO William K. Tasker by which we are offered a
       position as director of corporate communications for a company called Correct

We are romantics still, who stand and/or sit in shade

Looking straight down to the valley floor

Vertiginous, lofty, cerebral, lazy and tight

This poem may be recorded for quality assurance purposes

There we encounter planets whose colors we shall not forget

The Standard

The rock 'n' roll warehouse is opening its windows
What makes you say that?
You don't have to answer that
You could say Kikiribu Mandinga
You could say poetry publicity puberty probity
You could say wireless piano shoes
You can watch five different games while having a beer at JetBlue at Kennedy
The mind *is* the store, take it from me, open 24x7, universes streaming in parallel,
      which way do you like your eggs?
We're in crisis mode right now so stand by to remain calm
Words of the doorman, swing factor levels and dials, skinflint armchair, bone dry
      riverbed, make your way to the roof all ye who enter here

It's a mattress of interpretation
The heart goes west when interrupted
The freak stays in the picture
Similar to being on another planet
Only this time the image can fly
You have to write that down sometime but you don't have time what with your busy
      schedule because what you forget knows you like a picture tube being turned on
What does that tell you?
You got your head around it?
You were imprisoned by a picture, a picture of turbulence skillfully drawn by market
      requirements that shift in the wind of a bruised curiosity fleshed out and
      stammered and just there
Regulation letters forming ordinary words, food, drink, warmth, shelter, companionship,
      it's the same all over, that's life they say, and so it is, you take the good with the
      bad, the lines intersect, voices light up, it's time, here's yours

Books I Haven't Read Yet

Existential Honey from the Mind of a Strategist
The Voice of Things Asleep
The Book of Your Head
The Second Cage of Passion
Living on the Descent
The Distances of Arthur
Satanic Angels
The Waters of Seeing
The Well of Manhattan
Impressions of Crack Wars

Crash Again
Last Exit to the Sonnets
Gone in Search of Is
Our Nuclear Egotism
The Monkey's Wrench Stopped at the Promised Land Clapping the Sea
The Perfect Moment's Notice
Stones Against the Grain
The Power and the Passover
Materialism and the Little Fire Engine
The High Life and Hard Times of Chinese Hermits

Poem For Occupy

I'd like to give you a poem
That expresses all my hopes and fears
My anger and frustration with a world
Ruled by war, exploitation and social injustice
My desire for a better life
Awake to all being
Open to possibility
Free, spontaneous, caring
With respect for the earth
But I have not written such a poem
I cannot write it
Because I am only one person
And the words get stuck in my throat

The poem I am describing
Can only exist
When it is no longer mine
But has become the common property
Of all of us
Then our poem will be heard
Loud and clear
From the corridors of Wall Street
To Oscar Grant Plaza
And from Tahrir Square
To the polar icecaps
So that the world may revolve
Not around power and money
But with liberty and justice
For all in the light of the sun

Surplus Value

What in the end are mountains, rivers, earth, human beings, animals, and houses?

You turn the channel to view a life-size bust of Immanuel Kant draped in Mardi Gras beads, fuzzy dice, gold rope and kelp

A de-regulation of the senses has led to high-volume trading in category swaps, concept derivatives, 45's, 40's, 20's, BB's, A-rounds, zero-day vulnerabilities, negative capabilities, unreal numbers, rootkits, container cargo and junk in your trunk

And all because the word *valuosity* does not exist in the language of x's and o's

The Sunbeam Mixmaster Stand Mixer features a powerful 350-watt motor with 12 variable speeds for unsurpassed mixing versatility. Soft Start technology starts the motor slowly to prevent splatter

Flarf it up you flarfsters!

Unsurpassed, penetrating and perfect splatter is rarely met with, even in a hundred thousand million recording sessions

According to guitarist Myles Boisen, "We chose the name 'Splatter' because that's what we wanted the music to be like. Painterly, but also kind of bloody … half Pollock and half Peckenpah …"

According to Zen Master Dogen, "Making a living and producing things can be nothing other than giving"

Ain't no measuring stick involved at all

Direct Address

I think. How? By assuming it. I recall but poorly the speaker's corresponding coterie

Extreme pleasure, counting, other people's voices, an incredible sense of location, a

          center, a circumference, logic, narrative, scaffolding, rhymes, alphabet soup,

          short-term memory, modulation, strict formalism...

And on that note, tune in next week at the same time

One, two, three ... five, six, seven ... *enchufala, enchufala double ... dile que no*

And that's how we dance salsa, if by we we mean those of us who do, who do dance salsa

In writing one creates one's audience by believing in it

"Across time?" Why not? The conversational demi-monde of the New Narrative, the

          hyper-attentive devotees of Language Writing, the monk poets of old Japan, the

decadents

          of ancient Rome

Tonight, which is actually this morning, has arrived from New York, and then there's a

          time axis

And the same thing has happened from the title to the last line

But the poem is there

Mobile Iron

Stood all the way, packed in, one guy singing at the top of his lungs, along with, ear buds in,
some smiles, mostly not, we're all in this (car) together

Am I literally here? Is "this" a metaphor? When do relatives meet? For lunch? Be born every
day? Better to flip out than be bored? Better to see you with? Notify next of kin? If
your memory serves you well? Is this blue stop your blue stop?

Cranes, containers, buildings, trees – the primary landscape is planted, set into development
like rows

Looks like his uncle

Contextual clues reassure us we're on the right train, warn us away from deep crevices in the
earth, seams in our shifting states of mind

Perforated pages suggestive of short lists, groceries, emails and dates

Bound and determined to be

Looking for energy and finding it in the shadow of a smile, the casual gesture, the offhand
remark

Language as a stand-in for language underground

You have to laugh, and you do laugh, but the funny thing is, and the thing that is not so
funny also is, but not in the same way

Homenaje Para Ignacio Piñeiro

Rumba eh oy
Caminando
El montuno n'est-ce pa sale
Laissez les bontemps roulé
La rumba no es como ayer
Move the belt
Mulata! En tus ojos yo veo
The festival of the animals
En Afrique
Our ancestral home

My Home Is In A Southern Town

Progressing synchronically
up 12 frets
it's not what I play

It's what I don't play
I don't play an end
I see a bright world of infinite colors

The picture of a method
superimpositionally fraught
the iceberg is approaching Shaq

We dropped beats on the 100 ears
the line climbs up
like a series of freeze frames

In a hangar
background noise follows the contours of the dialectic
when it's sleepy time down South

In the space provided
by a body politic in a dread lock
every other odd encounter every day

The lash
the march
departure

Out of time
no eyes only ears and feet
the road tips

In a land of diaspora
a land of indefinite disintegrations
speedy book man

Glad to be unhappy
aboard stateless conveyances
transnational, supernumerary, persistent

Triumph Of The Underdog

for Charles Mingus

The western world
Is sad
A sad motherfucker
That takes everything it doesn't steal
You are no color
And were never born
O one who is was and will soon be

We are here
To do this thing
They call walkin' the dog
All up and down
The frickin' planet
To hell and back
So put on a jacket

No one knows
Where they will die
It's not even interesting
More to the point
Is gladiolus erectus
Nothing to sneeze at
Um-pa-pa Mexican music from out in a car

Sound is the structure
Classical modern or improvised what have you
This is composition
And marks the time
You breathe in and/or live in
If only to approach composure
While flying apart in the wind and the rain

The New Math

The cicadas are dining
On the circadian rhythms
Of scapular night

The train horn honks
A ways down the track
From here elasticity

A mixed bag
Lies in the corner
With nothing to say

One times one is one
The lone star number
Does zero one better

It's been real
But not so real
That we didn't get to chill

Thanks for that
The cool hat
Where you at?

I should think so
But don't
Because it's early yet

Mind over mattress
Billowing crowds
Familiar faces

Check mileage
Total acreage
Stan Brackage

You could say that
And you did
But not out loud

Cubicles are stacked
43 stories high
At One Market Plaza

For all the good
When see wave hi
It's *our* time

Love Shack

Word, image, sound, sense, feel, scene, take, give and go
Nothing can stop the Duke of Earl
Let go of everything and be where you are said the voice
The cherry blossoms arrive early in Washington this year
A gift from Japan one hundred years ago
In another generation they will open by February
Global warming is real
Nothing lasts forever
This heart of mine
Working in a coal mine

Backlog of caresses, murmurs and strokes
Tender shoots under spring clouds
Longing to put out, aching to give it up, jonesing to let it loose
No resting place but this one
Situated between islands
On a sea of absolute difference
Moving into range, pressing, pulling the covers off, leaping to one's feet
The journey takes months, takes weeks, hours, no more than 45 minutes
Get your ticket at the station
Scintillating light, strange light, light on prayer flags, twilight, cat on a cool
   wooden fence, ceanothus pushing up and out

The end is not literary
But expressive
Makes sense only in a flash
Immeasurably various in its manifestations
So concentrated as to appear bituminous

Sexually alert
Gives broad daylight a grin
Stands for no entity
Stands out against encompassing air

What Time Is It?

Through windows of crisis a new freedom
Resolved beyond jangling
Vinyasa cycles up the yin yang
Instead of practice we may choose therapy and/or drugs
Strange panels request non-existent authorization codes
On verges of wireless radio
Sea serpents hide sutras in undersea mountain caves
The whole she-bang is one bright pool
It is as necessary as it is one
Two interrupted nights in a row

11:58 AM – Winds WNW at 25 MPH. Noon is The Time of the Horse
Extra legroom costs $260
I'm still trying to peel myself off the floor/ceiling
Four-hour round-robin with execs popping in and out
A series of imaginary girls, all nattily attired, each labeled with a number indicating her age –
      3, 6, 1, 3, 8, 6, 10, 31, 70 (granma), etc.
Manage to get her to brush her teeth (I help)
As we detach carefully from the mother ship and float silently off into space
Who is doing what? And where are they? And who will be there? Did I miss anything? Is it
      happening now? In Chico? Choteau? Kyoto?
Sufficient unto the day is the funk thereof
As it is only ever now

For The Time Being

Time spills from the cup
There's more than enough
The past neither swallows the present
Nor pukes it forth
Each time is discrete
Yet continuous
Neither overlapping nor set apart
But just touching
In the moment between sucking wind
And blowing smoke

There is no permanent self
Because the self is a construct of phenomena being only for the time being
I may reach out to my younger self
With censure, irony or tenderness
But I cannot be him
Same with the older self, if any
Have yet to make his acquaintance
Which leaves what? This I
Watching atmospheric turbulence as wind whips trees' branches, leaves and flowers
Watching as I wait behind glass

Music Of The Common Tongue
for Christopher Small

Where are we exactly?

Looking at a map of the world like the back of our hand, in a book read by lamp light, in
       plain air overlooking "the" harbor

It's 10:49 AM in Santa Barbara, the bird does 47 different calls, hardly ever repeats, a
       total inventive genius!

Get back to what we were doing

A patient either is or is not on a table, put one foot in front of, pay no never mind, all
       that chatter, jive & yammer going on out there

Leaves always move about, air is, light on top, high-note palms, fanned out,
       separated instances of actuality

We arrive last night

We set the table using what's there, new information all the time, everything same but
       different, historical onions cut into tears and fried, more salt, a horizontal surface
       for keeping up

We wonder what's happening. Same-o same-o? Roll up vernacular shirt sleeves

Check it out

Whatever comes along goes along

Didn't someone in office say that?

A wide swath of color catches the eye and throws it into the pond where we will never
       find it

Like a light leak the massive intelligence behind every decision made to date gobbles up
       the scenery from one corner of the frame toward its center, where we can still
       make out the image of a commercial char grill under a faded black and grey
       plastic cover

Bird song is a kind of commentary but not one we can interpret literally

There is in every day the baffling principle of whatsis, pushing the living daylights out of
   the arranged marriage (heaven and hell), singular, bent on replication, yet
   wobbly, falling away from the remit

Work, shop, cook, pleasure, sadness, media, clothing, politics, art, philosophy, science
The natural world is a gas
We'd come back here anytime
There is, in communality, an emotional honesty, sometimes called "soul"

Keystone Corner

for Kathy Sloane

Words turn down the street
Turn down the lights
The sheets
Everyone says something
Speaking like this
Saying sometimes I get a little
Not depressed but mopey
Heard over sandwiches today
Or Basho on the road and sick
Saying I was feeling very low

From that place
Words move
As light moves
What it falls on
Into view
No news to you
An experienced observer
A practiced speaker
A denizen of the avenue
Totalling instants nearly as one

As song as envelope
Carries us along
From place to place
High and low
Affords views
Famous views
Ones commented on severally

By some of the greats
No kidding
It may be dark

It may be dank
And smoky in memory
And funky in memory
But the spirit opens out
But the spit shine stands out
When you put your tap shoes
Onto this evening's tattered shore
Just solid
Enough to feel
Under your own two feet

The Ragtime Skedaddlers

for Nick

Measures of succession
it gets dark
you notice a young

Woman pulling a small
white dog uphill
music from 100

Years ago resounds
white tile floor
fire engine wails

It's happening
and the curious mind tracks it
for the benefit of speech

A desire to express
not so much oneself
as the feeling of being alive

Tentative, painful and just
a dance across the decades
people then

Were just as they are now
only different
here's to the future

And there's the rub
aye, there's the rub
a moment in time

Awkward, poignant
whatever
while you were doing your laundry

Yeah
it's all good
tail lights in sequence

Rolling
of a darkening evening
up up

and on down the slope

Leaves Of Class

Plumes of smoke hang under a soft rain
As around town clouds and dogs and birds
Come up in here and thoughts well up and tears
And some strange kids climb carefully aboard carrying twenties
Salt tears of the sea rose keep on falling, waiting and waiting for spring to make land

Transparent fingers fondle tiny globes
Like giraffes they follow French curves of the pollen of map queens
Listing 17 reasons to visit the confidence mart
What reason could I give to you in the event?
Sleep in spring, springtime being what it is, giving everything

Everything always ultimately ends up otherwise
Walt had me at hello
I sign my name in glass and slide sideways
 "Una firma es acción, dos firmas son transacción" Luis Camnitzer
"A man signs a shovel and so he digs" Ted Berrigan

I'm sitting here with Derek Fisher talking about three great works: *The Straight Mind*,
        The Pacific War and "U.S. 1"
Tell me, Derek, can the Lakers repeat?
I repeat every day and it's not a transcript
These leaves of class stamp their signatures across our drawers for a lifetime of buoyancy
Suspenders *and* belts – leave nothing to chance

We return to our screens, the privately public, our respective devices, early and often
They await us like the shifting forms of dreams
Only now the speed-mad consolidation of global capital

Posts scores, stocks, weather, news, friends, filters, fuckers, flim-flam, flattery, fictive
      interlocutors, labile late arrivals, featured foodstuffs, ambient pill docks, branded
      skivvies, rumors of war, media buy-outs, parenting tips, nude chats, close shaves,
      long yardage, striped ties, expert testimony, striated imagery, words of comfort
      and helpful hints on the inner walls of our asylums
To hydrate our personas in case of drought

I wouldn't be here if it weren't for time
And I would like to personally thank the Timex Corporation for getting it right
OK let's take another look
The instant replay is a distortion, my God of course it looks like the player has
      possession, or doesn't, Zeno's paradox is the elephant in the room
Is there time in the time of your life?

Smoke blows holes in the argument, the arsenal, the exquisite poet blows smoke
The clouds and kids and birds arrive *en force*
Ever resident in emblematic ersatz auditoriums
Egged on by light-emitting dialectics
Moving surely, unhurriedly, into the darkest cabin of our welcoming heart

State Of The Onion

Nine squad cars parked outside the Joneses
Some days are better than others
Should I be more of a dandy?
Or shall I continue to "blend in"?
You look like your hair is on fire
They do run with scissors
63 = 3 x 3 x 7
Nine years in Evanston, nine in Cincinnati, four in New Haven and five in SF
Having now completed my third childhood
I look forward to switching trains at MacArthur Station

My new yellow stationery is perhaps too bright
Certainly for condolence notes
Possibly for any reason whatsoever
How rational shall we be in this stanza?
How non-rational the exciting surplus of people, places and things, all moving
    independently and veering interdependently, merging transactionally and
    dispersing desultorily
Cranes, containers, rail yards, parking, the bulk mail center where I worked once
Giants 7, Cardinals 5, red shirts and caps, orange ones
Is uniformity imposed from without? Or does it grow organically like a forest?
Should we paint a vision? Or win in trench warfare on features and functions?
The planet is getting hotter and so are you

In The American Room

Machine noise more than it lets on
Individuals, like widgets, are produced *en masse*
100 critics have other ideas
The feeling tone registers a disturbance
The *bocce* ball lands on the sand with an imaginary *thunk*
Birds and people have nothing in common, not even space
"It is my wicked will"
The day's work begins early and ends only when a sufficient amount of damage has been
        done
The world is absolutely independent of your tempers and moods, or is it?
In the American room, class is the elephant

In order to construct the City of God we must first kluge together a brain
Massive buildings frame the infrastructure of desire
No one can say exactly where the blue ball is now
Abashed at mythic overtones, flashing before the big screen
Each interval is open, every aspect of things can come into it
This moment is discrete
Existence can be said to sway slightly as if in a light wind
You bring to bear the experience of a lifetime as you slowly consume a slurpy
Two towels on a rail: sensuality
Instrumentality has its own sound, a vibration that is extra

Spiral Staircase

Why does that wall keep getting farther away?
A list with wheels
Chalk it up to the gap between living
Sunlight melts ice cubes in a tea
Relax and go with it

That's easy for you to say
You are not harnessed to an 18-ton behemoth on a global basis
But yes, we all breathe the same air
Says who?
Says the Master of Ballantrae

People Get Ready

after Curtis Mayfield

Where does poetry happen?
Between a "you" and a "me"
"Now We Are Six"
Is a poem by A.A. Milne
Now owned by Disney
The San Francisco Bay
Is now called "Oracle Bay"
But in the poem "Now We Are Six"
There is a "we"
And this "we" is like Whitman's "I"

A vehicle for shared experience
Like the country "America"
When it was presumed to exist
And therefore did exist in the imagination
As physical, spiritual force
And not simply as master brand
As it is now constituted in the media
So poetry moved inside
And went into private practice
Except in so far as the practice

Of poetry is inherently public
Being a formal arrangement of the common language of the tribe
Such that "she," "he" and "they" cannot help but get "it"
Thus poetry happens between and among people
However, it is an essentially solitary gig
So it also happens all the way inside

And you have to go there to find it
You can meet your friends there
And a lot of other interesting people, most of them nice
But sometimes there's no one home

And you have to sit there and look at a mostly empty parking lot
That's where poetry happens
In space
So if you are a space traveler
Zip up your space suit
And step into the poem
It is scheduled to arrive
At parts unknown
Every hour on the hour
And is picking up passengers
From coast to coast

Baseball

The infinite slowness of baseball
Nothing happens
What did you expect?
You can't smoke out there any more
That last pitch from Cain was pitch one hundred one

Rain falls on AT&T Park
7 Ks for Cain
And will fall here soon
We have plenty of time
Time is all around us after all

The rain falls like silk down
The single in the fifth inning was a bunt base hit
The crowd is thick, wet and happy
The ump flourishes his clicker
The right fielder kicks at the grass

The business of baseball changes
The dominant teams and faces certainly
Even their colors
But the game remains the fundamentally the same
On that you can rely – and be glad of it

Sandy

Seize the date
In plain view
Under the summit

You can't get there
Too much sudden water

What's new
Is also old with age
Collapsible buildings unfold

We used to say kind of
Now we say totally

People line up
To charge their cells
At a bank on 42nd

Four days cold dark
Is enough

Maybe you can stay
Uptown with friends
Until the power comes back on

Three Beautiful Americans

Arabic, Persian, Indonesian and Vietnamese
Are underserved
Macedonian, over

The crowd is the source
Professionals await you

The long tail of the digital dragon
Moves fast
Spells your name in page views

And the eyes have it
The eyeballs you buy up

Everyone wants to know your secret
Get rid of them all
But one

Behind the firewall
Or in the cloud

Local Timbre

Neighborhood sun smacks the head on straight, the weight, the pencil and its eraser, the
        question and its answer
Sounds amount to whatever it is out there, big bang, low motor, near bird, loud voice
I crack my face global, do you want me to *choose* these words? Politics is a numbers game
Socialism or barbarism, wrote Marx, wrote C.L.R. James
We're gonna pitch a wang dang doodle all night long, wrote Howlin' Wolf
The *is* that was
The *was* that wasn't
History branded, strapped, shipped
Who do you trust to tell you what really happened, what's really happening?
The fact of the matter isn't

In ungainly speech resides a spatial tub
Drawn to bathe the mind body in astral salts
Broken out of the jailhouse of metrical form
An image of Allen Ginsberg on every telephone pole
Hurtling toward history as this world goes wireless
Things mean nothing, I tell you
It's all in the writ
If light from the TV is reflected in a postcard to your left, flashing blue as CBS Sports
        cuts to a different angle, blue of Rafa's shirt, blue of the court, how fast can you
        open the door?
It all happens the moment you hit it, the moment you read it, write it
Sometimes when you write an autobiography you give away secrets like you don't like
        dogs, you don't like ham and cheese

Life is long. Art is squat. Diddly-squat. It gets better. Life, that is. As for art
The hardest part is after the opening
Your work sold but you strum your temples thinking only of those who didn't come
I didn't come all this way only to be put out to pasture, you think aloud

Little do you notice the subtle alternations of day and night, because you have Loud
    Brain Syndrome

Time to get back to the left margin, the last market, the list master, time to get out of the
    house, the paint, the box

You've spoken so coherently for so long it's surprising you haven't yet said everything
    there is to say, or have you?

Egad! I'm composing on screen! Whatever happened to climbing back up into the ear,
    when a year took forever and too many people were lined up for ice cream?

Yes, it's the same all over, but this time the pink squares are handing out vouchers to see
    the yellow diamonds turn the hotel upside down

And that's where we left off, only to rejoin the action, stressed to the max and half dead,
    though seemingly alert and relaxed

A foreign moon dusts the body with light, the height, the paper and its edge, solicitation
    and the pledge

Sights flash in the brain pan, evolution, plane noise, whose dog? whose big idea?

The date lays into history like a blank page, no words come to mind in the instant, the
    earth spins

The declarative sentence touches the rim of the world precisely nowhere

Or should I say everywhere? As we are unavoidably of it and have it in us and are no less
    ourselves

Does mathematics say nothing at all? People use it sometimes

I want to say that even the driest tautology is, as if despite itself, a form of human
    exposure

As is the framed instant of public language, flarf or con

Words blurb up like bulbs from soil

Nearby phenomena rehearse the customary flavors of an insistent bed of style

Stanzas In Medication

You wake up
You walk downstairs
Pull on a shirt
Pull sleep off of head
Put morning together

Later that night
Radio in other room
Thoughts tugging the attention
Then make tea
In among zones of light

A lamp is a glade
Tenderness arrives by stages
Rage won't let go
An inventory of accumulated sound
You wade into the swamp of words

Unexpected decompression
Sweep the walk
Husband your time
Plan long trips
A sight for soul eyes

Loud speakers
Sound bangs off walls
Who's in bed with
Learn to glide
Disappear into night

Confusing dreams
Wrong bed
Mid-field pile-up
Suit and tie, heavy dark-framed glasses
Wrong room

Muscles tight
Home delivery
Occupy words
Read the reports
Days work

Domesticatin' rhythm
Writ of have body
Red light in sound hole
Keep time alive
Say hi to friends on way out

London Olympic sadness
Something not something
Not something big
Something real
Like a glass of water on a window sill

No splash-o-meter
No shareholders
No peanut butter cups
Not enough light
Write it down anyway

Approaching zero
Remove hat size
Word sizzle
Account for shoes
Learn backwards news

Add Parisian atmosphere here
Bud mutters while he plays
He finds the walls
Loosely based on a long walk
See you back here later

Seven literary lions
Ate out at an automat
It was automatic writing all right
But which came first
The chicken or the road not taken

Lime-washed creamy whiteness
Sounds of construction everywhere
Brown frame shutters
In Brazil, Russia, India, China
Glare of purple earth

Time to rob billions on the strum lines
East-west incognito strike a pose
Last mean standing
Parable of the foot
You get what you cranked up to be

Walk a mile in my shoe size
Sea scavengers
Pussy Riot *in excelsis*
Devo: Don't roof-rack me, bro
Lines of sea made out of glass fractions

We have plenty of time to write this
Armature of sleep
Mind keeps producing what's real
Hit the skins or go to the bell
Our arms end in all hands on deck

The sea is a silent witness
Cognitive behavioral Theremin
Outside your ken
World keeps going
Joins up at intimate intersections

Time it takes to charge a phone
Rust on the torches
You think of those daffodils and totally chill
Soft clouds move inland
The day has parts watchmakers know from diddly

At Tom's Place

for Larry Ochs and Andrea Centazzo

In one music erase the adjustments

Sound comes on, I hear it well

I am the I who will

Great and green and revolving as all who might

Stop comparing yourself to others, that is, pay as much attention to others as you like
and give them their due, but reserve your greatest attention for your own work,
there and only there can any of this be worked out

Go deeper: seeds, birds, comfort, fields, tickets, spurs, diamonds, dirt, posters, flies,
sickness, air, fuel, dispatches, months, mentions, hairpins, larders,
pronunciations, stays, brickbats, tires, flourishes, administrations, carnivals,
snakes, oars, coins, temples, feet, decisions, harbors, treaties, props, dance steps,
jargon, hockey pucks, herbs, rocks, slime, odds, temperatures, coalitions, epochs,
confessions, territories, lies, sobs, birthmarks, deadlines, toasts, bugs, tunes,
baths, doctors, delights, ministries, potions, awards, shivers, bannisters,
problems, tear sheets, globules, interstices, curtains, baskets

Now that all that has been wrung out…

Not even relevant? Relevant to what?

It's a long night. With many stars in between

The information is a little, uh, sketchy

Music of words about music

Sound is my office and tuning the work of days. Nights I braid signals in an open pipe

Houston we have a glob

Who's that knockin'?

Celestial tea

Shimmering kind of, laid out across space

Penitentiary flim-flam

Erase the seams

Moon of the misbehavin'

It's only here, and you are only here to hear it, or not, or you are only there not to hear it,
  or only hear it not to be there. In any case, you undoubtedly are

Mr. Magoo meets Gerald McBoing Boing at the Rathskeller in Piscataway

Pretty Wombat

Balinese mumble-de-peg

Empty corridor, dawn light, sequencing retrospective ideas, only enough for one

Imaginary light, dial tone, hands free. Token resistance. Bedroll bathyscaphe.

  Thumb home

Y's Have A Way

Y's have a way of cozying up to you
The plastic mid-century, the silicon earway
Don't travel much in Amazonia anymore
In dreams we write the rules we were born to break
Voices signal the unseen other side of a dark fence
Push push, syntax is alive with urge, the human integer adding up to day
Air travel is all noise, the united flavors of time
You get it, you'll do it tomorrow you say
All decked out in the air of another matter, with every place to go

Black Tears

Thing copies end on emblems
Going fast from two-dollar facts
To 4x4 auto emissaries
Blink into dawn
Cheer the beachweather hillstands
Your birth status is exaggerated in earth shattering tone rows
Blink and the world blinks with you
Clean signs pop
Locus locali
Lean into the wind with your hand

Amazing gardens flow by your window
You are not you but an amalgam of other you's
Sensitivity fizzles in your fist
20/20 vision seals the deal
I'm trying to be as unassuming as possible
While still leaping tall buildings at a single bound here buddy
Virtuosity is just that – clean the filters
Speeches for players in movies
Lyrics for singers in out-of-the-way clubs
News items pulled from the feed of time

Error Message

Not even then
Piss-ant foreplay
Style sleeves
Lucky go five
Barely able to lift
Separated by coma
In a Latin spoon
Where heart rests
Gone down into
Bit and bright
Wool thesis
Parent tap open
Elements of dawn
Climb down marginalia
Are you set?

Similar to sizing
Tilting at pepper
What's missing stand up
Superimplosion
Borrowed feature
Meant nuts
One more leg en route
The body is the planet
Wa Wa & Co
Built to first
Idiom attic
One more cuppa
Spanglish jeans
Stone washed brain pan

Read your letter later
Parallel lives
Hoist ballast on deck
Drop over side
Cut through mimesis
Didn't get introduced
Self a smatter
A pill organizer almost
Lightning strikes thrice
Harrowing nifty and slight
Bottled up like
Paper get delivered
Flames erase a house
Sip glass reflex
Ordinary curvature day

Curvature of mind
Box set
Plead with, be done with
The hand that writes
Known at object relations
Objection handling
Set sail
Soon gone
Not home
Hammer sounds punctuate the day
Business is off the hook
Check my calendar
Door ajar
Known to hang out with
Set theory

Tomato differentiator
White flight pattern bald eagle
Take a breath mint coin operated
Simpler solutions exist
Come and bring the heat
Lime priority
Black power tool set foot
Put a jacket copy docudrama
More complex problems arise
Come and go in my wagon
Satsuma benefit
Red man chewing tobacco road
Sing a song bird watch face
Nothing is ever the same
Sound of the hills sung on the plain

Each point beads in a chain
Lemon verbena vortex
Leaning into the wind
I'll wait for you
Listen to that bird fly
Several seconds the least interval
Show what made of
Shower with affection
Always more where came from
Leave nothing out but this

Scope Creep

Synchronize your matches
Three on a light
Superstices
A shot in the dark
No such zone
Check for drone
You got me there
Which way to nowhere
An amazing trace
Fit for space
Seize on reading matter
Machine-woven jacket
Pen in head
Moving day
Simple syrup

Clouds dispense wisdom
Just a part of the story
Party of the third
Tails in full flight
No chorus, it's understood
Parallel lines leave ground
Stars fly apart
Form has only content to thank
And the content of our lives is what
Under construction
Until something false off a truck

Or personal injury
Whichever comes first
In which case we deal
One nation under clouds

Several seconds ago
No longer with us
I miss Gus!
He always seemed so present
An all-day event often ends evanescently
A series of a gone
Put the predicate
Release *every* from its prenomial mold
Get the hang of it
The tendency to drift
The subject slides out
Have one of mine
The social studies of a sunbeam
Correlate this
Nothing that is not given

Not sure what to make of
Suggest another bullet
Don't tease me
Simple rollouts
Green is the color of
Tempting to take it
The louche entry
When it's sleepy time down south
All but forgotten

Not bad for an after thought
Careening between walls
The dutiful sentiment
Large as a moose head
Subject to fits
Long enough to last

Lasting away
At the Apple store about to pass out
Passwords are scars
Clowns pile out of tiny car
To park is to neck
Flecks of color
Easy to love
Radio silex
Happy to serve you
Life of a salesperson
Too white to be
Whiling the time
Integration specialist
Packed house
As when we go out on a limb

One big system
Wait a minute
Being part of
Is of the moment
And in a moment
The door hinges blobward
Because anything can happen

Between and among molecules

So that the connective tissue

Becomes the whole story

Continuity playing with interruption

Until Proust pastes in the latest insertion

And the sentence expands to fill a cartoon forest

With empty thought balloons

That pop in thin air

On the outskirts of associated writing pogroms

Filtered heads roll lengthwise in a blustery crouch

Often not mentioning repeated offenses under the bell tower's watchful I-beam

A lighter lights up an alley at night in the rain

What rain is that? The fingers gain purchase on the limit case, the edge case

We don't have to show you our stinking badges

Satisfaction while you're up, situation down under the ground, suggestion box flavors
    rising to fever pitch

A copy of the article is sitting on your desk waiting to surprise you when you get back
    from vacation

Long lead times make strange bedfellows

The muscles hug the bones for the big push-off

Against sleep we have only this worn mask, a play on goat song carried too far, a red lack

Somewhere else is the right place to be, you can write in about it later, meanwhile keep a
    low profile, smoke sparingly

There are trails up into the interior or down to the sea it makes no difference

The sky trembles with emotional weight-training for the gods, the special gift of Franz
    Boaz, anthropologist to the gods

Eventually everyone ends up unconscious, even if evening enters an empty alternate
    universe attached as eyes of affability

Parallel Play

What's your worldview say?
Joint paint?
Collapsed solids for a day
Spread thickness in air war
Columnar data is big

Time? What's time?
None too blownpast, ain't it?
Serial book reads eyeballs
During forest fire in church
Hallelujah sasparilla fashionista

Aerial mowing frequents
Bad car money in the pines
Every time we look we find nada
Mentions line up like stays
Cut the house in half and leave it be

Taps

Before turning everything off
Remember to finish the century
A lie to them who would tell it
Simplifying nothing
In favor of pulling up strokes
So may the dawn be lit
With favorable indicators
Pressed into the streets like rain
After burning the last tree standing
Walk up to the ocean and spit

Seven, eight times from now
Everything will be different
Line of cars pulled up to a drawbridge
Migratory birds in flight, rubber
Serpentine crease aglow in a riverbed
Almost lost, seriously far off course
When posing questions, sleep soundly
That doesn't make any sense
Not to worry, the information bus is late
Spectacular autumn sentinels dust the west

Tan Notebook

9/6/11

"… ragged diabolical incoherences uninvitedly reccurring to me… I promise nothing complete; because any human thing supposed to be complete, must for that very reason infallibly be faulty."
Herman Melville, *Moby Dick* (193)

12/15

"Irritable reaching" (Keats). After that feeling – neurotransmitters. Or that connection – social networking. Something coming in from outside. But isn't something always coming in from outside? If you can stay quiet enough to notice.

Time is all. More nitty gritty than you can shake a stick at. When on the edge of it, everything seems to empty out. Watch that first step!

An illusion produced by anxiety. What are you worried about? The defective hoodlum in the film noir (*The Enforcer*, 1952), "going to pieces." That you won't make deadline? Run out of time? Wind up dead?

"Time is all around us," as the Magsaysay informed cris cheek. As children know and demonstrate without effort.

12/16

Write operations are optimistic. This is the cutting edge and flash is the blade.

12/18

We swim thru a 3D grid of signals. Radio everywhere. The air is the message. Subtracted from content.

12/19

Casting a sidelong glance.

It's 3:03 pm, December 19, 2011. The sun is already low in the sky, the other side of the Bay. But now I am underground, 19th Street Oakland station. "The final destination of this train is San Francisco." The documentary life.

People consult their devices. Left to their own. When we surface at West Oakland, I'll check to see when tonight's football game starts.

Now I'm coming back the other way, and the game I mentioned before is under way.

12/20

Game delay. Antiquated infrastructure. The lights at Candlestick cut out. Twice in the first half. How to keep warm on the sidelines.

I dreamt I was in a restaurant, the kind of place that caters to tourists and conventioneers, and I was very tired, I didn't care about the food, I just wanted to sleep. Whereupon I woke up and couldn't get back to sleep for an hour and a half.

Our stove wouldn't light. Quan came and replaced the igniter.

Amy Winehouse lives.

12/21

Winder solstice. Days get longer? More daylight to search for a bass player. More time to pry apart the dependencies, the contingencies, the interlocking directorates, the diminished chords, the table stakes, the interstices, the dayparts, the to-do's, the station stops, the meeting requests, the web posts, the drinks, the books, the tracks, the cuts, the family members, the personalities, the random thoughts, the houses, the apartments, the streets and roads, the hospitals and schools, the states, the nation states, the continents, the oceans, the constellations and the clouds. To pry them apart and enter, there to inhabit, here to write it all down.

12/29

Things happen. Hospitalizations, legal threats, layoffs, loan rejections, the list is literal, literal fact. Games and music wrap around the eventual facts of life, the evidentiary plumage of calvacades wending into aether. Way pleasant is this simple hidebound release, especially packed in sound, the random registrations of night. The reckless luminosity standing perfectly upright and still.

12/31

Last night of the year. Space pulls down its drawers. The ambient winds play Misty. Long flute lines wind around the block. The scene is set, the set demolished. You have only to go on your system, nervous. One hit of home before you go.

1/1/12

Football espresso flute edge sunlight day. New Year's Irresolutions. The great wheel of the year begins slowly to turn.

1/2

It's your turn. Up in the morning and off to school. The school of hard clocks. Dreaming of seeing. Seeing a ball get lost among leaves in a forest. A first time for everything. A fine rain only in the mind. Left-handed brain drain. Left for dead yet still kicking. Open the gate.

Swim like a mammal.

"Turning right at Nihonmatsu, we had a quick look at the cave of Kurozuka and walked on to spend the night at Fukushima."
Basho, "The Narrow Road through the Provinces" (1689), trans. Earl Miner, *Japanese Poetic Diaries* (166)

1/9

Not too long ago I wrote the following word: stubble. They have a setting on the shaver where you can keep it just like that while reading your Bible. Sometimes I think one word and write another. Only to discover my mistake moments later when I read what I have written. Before I send it, I try to make sure it's ok. The contours of speech trace the body of the tribe. I love it.

1/16

Silence. The street, the city hums. Reclining at the back end of a mood swing. Hung up. Stranded. Shit out of luck. Nothing but a man.

"Three nineteen! … three nineteen," barks Aaron Rodgers, and Packers go down to ignominious defeat. But the victorious Giants will have to face the 49ers at Candlestick next weekend in the rain.

"For today's tourist, orientation is impossible."
Rimbaud, *Illuminations*, trans. John Ashbery (89)

1/17

Long trains of memories, dreams and constructions course through the night on rails of breathing. Groups of humans gather inside great halls for dancing and sex. Drugs keep them up until 6 AM in the parking lot. Grace Jones joins them, feeling her way toward dawn. The weekend opens up into one endless day, which in turn devours the week. Looking back, the survivors have dodged a bullet. Now they are content to merely be.

1/19

"Sometimes you have to pull in the oars and lie down in the boat."
Tala's tai-chi teacher

1/22

"There were islands beyond counting, some tall ones pointing each its finger toward the sky, the other lower ones crawling on their bellies across the sea."
Basho at Matsushima (Miner, 173)

"The next morning we set out once again on random travel over unknown roads."
Basho (Miner, 175)

1/23

"There was not so much as a sound."
Basho (Miner, 180)

1/28

Dream message in French:

Meme s'il faut que tout mourit, un doit essayer.

1/29

WRITING ACROSS FOUR NOTEBOOKS

Writing in pencil is how one does it in music so as to erase when necessary making
      adjustments as one goes
The sound of the violin comes over the airwaves I have the radio on I have time
Where I get off is the next stop but who knows when we will reach the station
Meanwhile all is as you might not suspect luminous green rapidly rotating and
      revolving around the sun great provider of light and heat

1/31

In a tall office building, near the top floor. Plush carpets, cubicles, law books, hardwood. It's the executive suite, I know, having worked there once. Looking for the men's room.

Can't find. Looking for an elevator. Take escalator instead. Escalator is huge, flat, tilted downward, no stairs, endless and very fast. Think Leningrad Metro. Without cutting back, how can it descend the whole height of the building? The geometry doesn't work.

Hit the basement. A vast entertainment emporium for the masses. Singers, dancers, acts, games, prizes. They're lined up to shoot baskets, three for a quarter. Then actual games going on. I consider joining in, think better of it. Then a group of women laughing and talking, familiar, and stairs leading up, but it's a women's spa of some kind, not for me.

Back the other way, a huge bar and restaurant. Feeling hung over, I decide to order a bloody Mary, maybe crab, or tuna, scanning the board for fish, most entries are missing, designated only by pins. Wondering about luggage, I seem to be on the brink of departure.

2/1

Your prose has a tie on.

2/6

Read these words you members of a future time
And know the one who wrote them is not one of you
But still that you are surely of that one descended
Since you perceive a voice in these bare lines

2/9

THE RAINBOW JUMPER OF PURVIS SHORT

Something that sweet
Had to cook a long time

2/10

"Why travel? You'll only come back."
Jean Cocteau, *Les dames du Bois de Boulogne*, dir. Robert Bresson (1949)

2/14

Take a page out of somebody else's book
In between sleep and that other state, what do they call it?

2/20

SENCHA

Small fire at late afternoon hut
Light touching pink blossoms
Much is done and gone
Much more is yet to be
An orange amid dark leaves

2/22

We can throw the sports bra and the broom out together
Then we will have to get new ones

2/29

"Flawless, on a Monday."
Joshua Gamson, *The Fabulous Sylvester* (272)

3/1

"After a time the assembly bell rang for breakfast, and I joined the priests in their dining
hall. Thinking that I had to get into Echizen Province today, I felt rather in a hurry,
but as I started down the steps from the dining hall, young priests crowded about me,
holding onto paper and an inkstone. It happened to be the time when the willows of the
temple garden were dropping their leaves, so I wrote:

    The willow leaves fall –
After sweeping the temple garden
      I hope I can leave

"Anxious to get on, I just scribbled it down, as is my sandals were already in motion."
Basho (Miner, 192)

3/8
"As charged particles slam the earth's magnetic field at more than a million miles per hour and are funneled toward the north and south poles, they generate the nighttime light known as auroras or northern and southern lights."
Kenneth Chang, "Solar Bursts Spray Earth, With More to Come," *New York Times*, 3/8/12

3/14

Water from sky
Lands on earth
In an imagination of seeming

3/20

"The eyes are the windows of the soul."
Wittgenstein quoted by Alec Guinness as Professor Marcus in *The Ladykillers* (1955)

3/27

Sufficient unto the day is the funk thereof
As it is only ever now

About the Author

KIT ROBINSON was born in Evanston, Illinois, grew up in Cincinnati, attended Yale University, and has lived in the San Francisco Bay Area ever since. He is the author of *Marine Layer* (BlazeVOX), *Catalan Passages* (Streets and Roads), *Determination* (Cuneiform), *The Messianic Trees: Selected Poems, 1976-2003* (Adventures in Poetry), and many other books of poetry, including collaborations with Ted Greenwald, *A Mammal of Style* (Roof) and *Takeaway* (c_L Books).

About CHAX

Founded in 1984 in Tucson, Arizona, Chax has published 200 books in a variety of formats, including hand printed letterpress books and chapbooks, hybrid chapbooks, book arts editions, and trade paperback editions such as the book you are holding. In August 2014 Chax moved to Victoria, Texas, and is presently located in the University of Houston-Victoria Center for the Arts, which has generously supported the publication of *An Intermittent Music*, which has also received support from many friends of the press. Chax is an independent 501(c)(3) organization which depends on support from various government and private funders, and, primarily, from individual donors and readers.

Recent and current books-in-progress include *The Complete Light Poems*, by Jackson Mac Low, *Life–list*, by Jessica Smith, *Andalusia*, by Susan Thackrey, *Diesel Hand*, by Nico Vassilakis, *Dark Ladies*, by Steve McCaffery, *What We Do*, by Michael Gottlieb, *Limerence*, by Saba Razvi, *Short Course*, by Ted Greenwald and Charles Bernstein, *An Intermittent Music*, by Ted Pearson, *Arrive on Wave*, by Gil Ott, *Entangled Bank*, by James Sherry, *Autocinema*, by Gaspar Orozco, *The Letters of Carla, the letter b.*, by Benjamin Hollander, *A Mere Ica*, by Linh Dinh, *A Night in the Sun*, by Will Alexander, and *Visible Instruments*, by Michael Kelleher.

You may find CHAX online at http://chax.org